My Rock and My Salvation

25 Encouraging Scriptures and Prayers

ONE NEIGHBOR
PUBLISHING

Front cover image by Unsplash (@Winngo Tse) (@Quino Al).
Book design by Studio 7.

First printing edition 2024.

One Neighbor Publishing
1333 Buckeye Avenue #1019
Ames, Iowa 50010

For you.

PREFACE

As you know being a Christian is more than just accepting Jesus as your Savior in a prayer. It's a relationship; spending time and getting to know God for who He is. God is our Father in Heaven, Creator, Savior, Protector, anything that we need God has got it.

God placed it on my heart to prepare this group of Scriptures and prayers. Read one Scripture and pray the accompanying prayer each day (aloud, if you can, even if it is just a whisper). There is power in our spoken word. This Scripture-prayer pairing is known as praying the Scriptures or praying God's Word back to Him. It's an effective way of praying and getting prayers answered.

I pray these Scriptures encourage, strengthen, and draw you closer to God the Father. You will not regret it.

In His Service,

Tyson Canty

DAY 1

Deuteronomy 31:6
Be strong and courageous, do not be afraid or in dread of them, for the Lord your God is the One who is going with you. He will not desert you or abandon you.

Lord, help me to be strong and courageous. I will not be afraid or dread because You are with me. Your Word says, You will not desert me or abandon me. Thank You for this promise. In Jesus's name, amen.

DAY 2

Psalms 62:6-8

He alone is my rock and my salvation, my refuge; I will not be shaken. 7 My salvation and my glory rest on God; the rock of my strength, my refuge is in God. 8 Trust in Him at all times, you people; pour out your hearts before Him; God is a refuge for us. Selah

Lord, You alone are my rock and my salvation, my refuge. Nothing can shake my faith and trust in You. My rescue, help, salvation including any praise and honor I receive comes from You. You are the source of my strength and my place of safety. I trust in You. Protect me from all afflictions and rescue me. In Jesus's name, amen.

DAY 3

Malachi 4:2
But for you who fear My name, the sun of righteousness will rise with healing in its wings; and you will go forth and frolic like calves from the stall.

Lord, I fear and reverence Your name. In Your presence there is healing. Show me favor and I will be blessed with youthful energy and health. In Jesus's name, amen.

DAY 4

Exodus 14:14
The Lord will fight for you, while you keep silent.

Lord, even in my silence, You fight for me. Thank You, for warring and winning in my favor. In Jesus's name, amen.

DAY 5

Proverbs 3:5-6

Trust in the Lord with all your heart and do not lean on your own understanding. 6 In all your ways acknowledge Him, and He will make your paths straight.

Lord, I trust You with all my heart even in the things I do not understand for Your ways and thoughts are not like mine. In everything I do, I acknowledge You as my God. Guide me and keep me from falling. In Jesus's name, amen.

DAY 6

Isaiah 58:8-9

Then your light will break out like the dawn, And your recovery will spring up quickly; And your righteousness will go before you; The glory of the Lord will be your rear guard. 9 Then you will call, and the Lord will answer; You will cry for help, and He will say, 'Here I am.'If you remove the yoke from your midst, The pointing of the finger and speaking wickedness,

Lord, Your light and presence overcomes the darkness. My recovery will not tarry as I walk in right standing with You. Help me to be in right standing with You. Your glory will shield and protect me and from whatever I cannot see that means me harm. I call on You and You answer. I lay down my burdens before You that do not profit my spirit and soul. Free me from whatever hinders me from living for you. Change my speech, restore my voice, and align my thoughts away from blame or guilt. In Jesus's name, amen.

DAY 7

Matthew 17:20

And He said to them, "Because of your meager faith; for truly I say to you, if you have faith the size of a mustard seed, you will say to this mountain, 'Move from here to there,' and it will move; and nothing will be impossible for you."

Lord, grow my faith. I declare my faith is bigger than a mustard seed. I say to the mountain (call out what is standing in your way) before me, "Move. I command every hindrance and obstacle be laid low and cast into the sea." Nothing is too hard or impossible for You, God. In Jesus's name, amen.

DAY 8

James 1:3
Knowing that the testing of your faith produces endurance.

Lord, may this testing of my faith produce endurance. May I not get weary or tired. I declare victory is my portion. Strengthen me with Your joy and power. In Jesus's name, amen.

DAY 9

Hebrews 11:1
Now faith is the certainty of things hoped for, a proof of things not seen.

Lord, let my faith be evidence of my hope in You. I will walk by faith and not by sight. What I see with my eyes has no bearing on what You are doing in the spirit. I praise You for what You have done, are doing, and will do. In Jesus's name, amen.

DAY 10

Psalms 121:1-2
I will raise my eyes to the mountains; from where will my help come? 2 My help comes from the Lord, Who made heaven and earth.

Lord, You made heaven and earth. Your power is limitless. Your arm is never too short to reach me. My help comes from You, and You alone. Help me keep my eyes on You and not on what surrounds me. In Jesus's name, amen.

DAY 11

Jeremiah 29:11
For I know the plans that I have for you,' declares the Lord, 'plans for prosperity and not for disaster, to give you a future and a hope.

Lord, I trust the plans You have for me. Your plans include my prosperity in mind, body, and spirit, and not disaster or loss of any kind. I come against all events and circumstances in my life that disrupt Your plans for me, in Jesus's name. I declare my mind and eyesight flourishes with clarity and focus. I declare my body is restored and healthy. I declare my spirit is strong and steadfast in You. In Jesus's name, amen.

DAY 12

Psalms 73:26
My flesh and my heart may fail, but God is the strength of my heart and my portion forever.

Father God, though I am mortal and have weaknesses, You do not hold them against me. Your grace and mercy cover me when I am weak and unsure. I acknowledge Your glory and might. You never sleep so nothing catches You off guard. You can not lie because You are Truth. You will never fail because You are victorious in all Your exploits. You are my strength and my faith lies in You. You are my God and my inheritance through the sacrifice of Your son. Keep my mind stayed on You. In Jesus's name, amen.

DAY 13

Psalms 55:22
Cast your burden upon the Lord and He will sustain you; He will never allow the righteous to be shaken.

Lord, I cast my burdens, my worries, and pain upon You. Cleanse my heart and mind of all that is unrighteous, that I might be acceptable in Your sight. I surrender to You. Strengthen and comfort my heart. Your Word says, You will never allow the righteous to be shaken. Though everything around me may shake, let me stand firm on Your Word and be victorious. In Jesus's name, amen.

DAY 14

1 Peter 5:7
Having cast all your anxiety on Him, because He cares about you.

Lord, I give You all my anxiety and fears. Increase my faith and show me Your great love for me. I know without any doubt that You care about me. You have numbered the hairs on my head and my days. Help me to rest, knowing there is no safer place to be than in Your hand. In Jesus's name, amen.

DAY 15

Psalms 56:3
When I am afraid, I will put my trust in You.

Lord, when I am afraid, remind me that You will never leave me nor abandon me. You are always by my side. I put my trust in You. In Jesus's name, amen.

DAY 16

2 Corinthians 12:9
And He has said to me, "My grace is sufficient for you, for power is perfected in weakness." Most gladly, therefore, I will rather boast about my weaknesses, so that the power of Christ may dwell in me.

Lord, though I have good days and bad days, Your grace is enough. It is in my weakness that Your power is perfected. I will tell everyone of Your goodness in the midst of my weakness, that Your power and love may be seen by all. In Jesus's name, amen.

DAY 17

Matthew 10:30-31

But even the hairs of your head are all counted. 31 So do not fear; you are more valuable than a great number of sparrows.

Lord, You know how many hairs I have on my head. You made me and molded me. You know every intricate detail and all the inner workings of my body. I am not worried. I know that I am the apple of your eye. The price Jesus paid on the cross demonstrates my worth is far above that of sparrows. I stand on the authority of the blood of Christ and destroy all anomalies in my body that go against the blueprint and plans of God. In Jesus's name, amen.

DAY 18

Psalms 61:1-2

Hear my cry, God; give Your attention to my prayer. 2 From the end of the earth I call to You when my heart is faint; lead me to the rock that is higher than I.

Lord, hear my prayer. I know You hear me when I call out to You. There is no place I can go that You can not hear me. When my faith is weak and my strength is drained, lead me back to sit in Your presence so that You can rejuvenate and re-energize me. You are my rock and nothing by any means can harm me. In Jesus's name, amen.

DAY 19

Isaiah 41:10
Do not fear, for I am with you; do not be afraid, for I am your God. I will strengthen you, I will also help you, I will also uphold you with My righteous right hand.'

Lord, You are my God. There is none like You. I am not fearful of the obstacles that I can see nor the unknown because You are with me. Strengthen me, Father God. Help me today. Place me and keep me on the path of righteousness. In Jesus' name, amen.

DAY 20

John 11:25-26

Jesus said to her, "I am the resurrection and the life; the one who believes in Me will live, even if he dies, 26 and everyone who lives and believes in Me will never die. Do you believe this?

Lord Jesus, I believe You are the Son of God, that You died on the cross for my sins, and rose again after three days. In You there is eternal life because You are the resurrection. I believe that in You there is only life, even in death. In Jesus's name, amen.

DAY 21

2 Corinthians 12:8-10

Concerning this I pleaded with the Lord three times that it might leave me. 9 And He has said to me, "My grace is sufficient for you, for power is perfected in weakness." Most gladly, therefore, I will rather boast about my weaknesses, so that the power of Christ may dwell in me. 10 Therefore I delight in weaknesses, in insults, in distresses, in persecutions, in difficulties, in behalf of Christ; for when I am weak, then I am strong.

Lord, I know Your ways are not like mine and Your thoughts are not like mine. I may never know why some see miracles and others do not. You have a plan and purpose for us all. Regardless of how things look, I am still hopeful, faithful, and persistent that your plan and purpose will be fulfilled in my life. I will continue to delight in my difficulties knowing that these too shall pass. May Your power that dwells in me make me strong. I declare I have the victory in Jesus's name, amen.

DAY 22

Psalm 46:10a
Stop striving and know that I am God;

Lord, help me not to fight against You, but fight alongside You. You have my best interest at heart and plans to bless me, not harm me. You already know the end from the beginning. I trust in You because You know all and are all-powerful. Help me not to ever forget that You are God. In Jesus's name, amen.

DAY 23

2 Corinthians 4:16-18
Therefore we do not lose heart, but though our outer person is decaying, yet our inner person is being renewed day by day. 17 For our momentary, light affliction is producing for us an eternal weight of glory far beyond all comparison, 18 while we look not at the things which are seen, but at the things which are not seen; for the things which are seen are temporal, but the things which are not seen are eternal.

Lord, help me to remember that though my body ages daily, my spirit will live forever. Renew my spirit daily. Whatever sickness I may be enduring, it will produce good fruit in me. Help me to see with my spiritual eyes the things You have for me. I declare I am getting stronger, my faith is increasing, my peace is from You, and nothing can compare to the eternal glory promised me. In Jesus's name, amen.

DAY 24

Ephesians 3:20-21
Now to Him who is able to do far more abundantly beyond all that we ask or think, according to the power that works within us, 21 to Him be the glory in the church and in Christ Jesus to all generations forever and ever. Amen.

Lord, You are capable (and want) to do far more and beyond whatever I ask or think, according to Your power that works within me. Please move in my life and do what You will. To You, God, be the glory and honor in the church in Christ Jesus forever and ever. Amen.

DAY 25

Romans 15:13

13 Now may the God of hope fill you with all joy and peace in believing, so that you will abound in hope by the power of the Holy Spirit.

Lord, my hope lies in You. Fill me with all joy and peace in believing so that I will overflow in hope by the power of the Holy Spirit. In Jesus's name, amen.

www.ingramcontent.com/pod-product-compliance
Lightning Source LLC
Chambersburg PA
CBHW082113120626
46553CB00011B/3669